The Teacher's Pocket Guide to Questioning

By Mike Gershon

Text Copyright © 2018 Mike Gershon

All Rights Reserved

About the Author

Mike Gershon is known in the United Kingdom and beyond as an expert educationalist whose knowledge of teaching and learning is rooted in classroom practice. His online teaching tools have been viewed and downloaded more than 3.5 million times, making them some of the most popular of all time.

He is the author of over 100 books and guides covering different areas of teaching and learning. Some of Mike's bestsellers include books on assessment for learning, questioning, differentiation, growth mindsets and stretch and challenge. You can train with Mike online, from anywhere in the world, via TES Institute. He regularly delivers CPD and INSET in schools across the UK and Europe.

Find out more at www.mikegershon.com

Training and Consultancy

Mike offers a range of training and consultancy service covering all areas of teaching and learning, raising achievement and classroom practice. Examples of recent training events include:

- Using Growth Mindsets to Develop Resilient Learners

- AfL Unlocked: Practical Strategies for Classroom Success

- Stretching and Challenging More-Able Learners

- Effective Questioning: Developing a Toolkit of Strategies to Raise Achievement

- Differentiating for Whole-Class Teaching

To find out more, visit:

www.mikegershon.com

www.gershongrowthmindsets.com

Or get in touch via mike@mikegershon.com

Other Works from the Same Author

Available to buy now on Amazon:

The Teaching Assistant's Pocket Guide Series:

The Teaching Assistant's Pocket Guide to Growth Mindsets

The Teaching Assistant's Pocket Guide to Questioning

The Teaching Assistant's Pocket Guide to Feedback

The Teaching Assistant's Pocket Guide to Differentiation

The Teaching Assistant's Pocket Guide to Assessment for Learning

The Teaching Assistant's Pocket Guide to Supporting Less-Able Learners

The Teaching Assistant's Pocket Guide to Positive Behaviour Management

The Teaching Assistant's Pocket Guide to Metacognition

The Teaching Assistant's Pocket Guide to Supporting EAL Learners

The Teaching Assistant's Pocket Guide to Teaching and Learning

The 'How To…' Series:

How to use Differentiation in the Classroom: The Complete Guide

How to use Assessment for Learning in the Classroom: The Complete Guide

How to use Bloom's Taxonomy in the Classroom: The Complete Guide

How to use Questioning in the Classroom: The Complete Guide

How to Develop Growth Mindsets in the Classroom: The Complete Guide

How to use Discussion in the Classroom: The Complete Guide

How to Manage Behaviour in the Classroom: The Complete Guide

How to Teach EAL Students in the Classroom: The Complete Guide

How to use Feedback in the Classroom: The Complete Guide

How to be an Outstanding Trainee Teacher: The Complete Guide

The 'Quick 50' Series:

50 Quick Ways to Stretch and Challenge More-Able Students

50 Quick Ways to Create Independent Learners

50 Quick Ways to go from Good to Outstanding

50 Quick Ways to Support Less-Able Learners

50 Quick Ways to Get Past 'I Don't Know'

50 Quick Ways to Start Your Lesson with a Bang!

50 Quick Ways to Improve Literacy Across the Curriculum

50 Quick Ways to Improve Feedback and Marking

50 Quick and Brilliant Teaching Ideas

50 Quick and Brilliant Teaching Techniques

50 Quick and Easy Lesson Activities

50 Quick and Ways to Help Your Students Secure A and B Grades at GCSE

50 Quick and Ways to Help Your Students Think, Learn and Use Their Brains Brilliantly

50 Quick Ways to Motivate and Engage Your Students

50 Quick Ways to Outstanding Teaching

50 Quick Ways to Perfect Behaviour Management

50 Quick and Brilliant Teaching Games

50 Quick and Easy Ways Leaders Can Prepare for Ofsted

50 Quick and Easy Ways to Outstanding Group Work

50 Quick and Easy Ways to Prepare for Ofsted

50 Quick and Easy Ways to Outstanding English Teaching (with Lizi Summers)

50 Quick and Brilliant Ideas for English Teaching (with Lizi Summers)

50 Quick and Easy Ways to Build Resilience through English Teaching (with Lizi Summers)

Other Books:

More Secondary Starters and Plenaries

Secondary Starters and Plenaries: History

How to be Outstanding in the Classroom

Teach Now! History: Becoming a Great History Teacher

The Exams, Tests and Revision Pocketbook

The Growth Mindset Pocketbook (with Professor Barry Hymer)

Series Introduction

The 'Teaching Assistant's Pocket Guide' series developed out of my desire to give teaching assistants across the country a set of practical, useful books they could call on to help them in their work. Having worked with teaching assistants throughout my teaching career and knowing full well the hugely positive impact they can have on learners in a whole variety of different classrooms, I thought it was high time there was a series of books dedicated to supporting them in their working lives.

Each volume in the series focuses on a different aspect of teaching and learning. Each one aims to give teaching assistants a quick, easy way into the topic, along with a wide range of practical strategies and techniques they can use to support, guide and develop the learners with whom they work.

All of the books are designed to help teaching assistants. Each one goes out of its way to make their lives easier, and to help them develop professionally. But, crucially, the ultimate aim of each book is to give teaching assistants the tools they need to better support the learners they spend their time working with.

The whole series is written with the classroom in mind. This is a collection practical of books for what is a practical job.

I hope you find the series useful, interesting and informative. I hope it helps you to develop your work in the classroom and, of course, I hope it helps you to work ever more effectively with your learners on a daily basis.

Acknowledgements

My thanks to all the staff and students I have worked with past and present, including all the teachers and teaching assistants, particularly those at Pimlico Academy and King Edward VI School, Bury St Edmunds. Thanks also to the teachers and teaching assistants who have attended my training sessions and who always offer great insights into what works in the classroom. Finally, thanks to Kall Kwik BSE for their great design work and thanks also to the Education Endowment Foundation for their illuminating research on the role of teaching assistants.

Table of Contents

Chapter 1 – What's in a question?..12

Chapter 2 – Opening Up Learner Thinking........................20

Chapter 3 – Getting Past 'I Don't Know'..............................30

Chapter 4 – How to Get Better Responses 39

Chapter 5 – Scaffolding Questions 48

Chapter 6 – Open vs Closed Questions.............................57

Chapter 7 – Creative Questioning Techniques 66

Chapter 8 – Bloom's Taxonomy Questioning.....................75

Chapter 9 – SOLO Taxonomy Questioning........................85

Chapter 10 – Conclusion – Recapping and Next Steps ...93

Select Bibliography..98

Chapter 1 – What's in a question?

We ask questions all the time in the classroom. They are one of the main ways we communicate with learners. Questions help us influence learners' thinking. To send their thoughts in certain directions. They help us to open up their imaginations, to change their minds and to push them to go beyond what they can already do.

This book is all about how you can ask better questions.

How you can grow and develop your questioning techniques and strategies.

Good questions lead to high-quality thinking. And that leads to great progress.

The better our questions, the better learning we set up for our learners.

So, what's in a question? Or, to put it another way, how do questions work? What do they do and what makes one question better than another?

Let's start to explore this by looking at some different questions. For each one, I'd like you to take a moment to imagine what your response might be. Don't think about it too much. Just imagine that someone you know asked you the question. How would you respond?

1) What happened in the match?

2) Did we win?

3) Where do we go from here?

4) What if you had a different hat you could wear?

5) How many people do you know?

6) How many people do you really know?

7) Where do you think learning happens?

8) Can you define learning?

9) Is it ever right to lie?

10) How much?

I imagine your responses to each question were different. This is because the questions are different. But they all share a common theme. Something common to every question that is asked. It's this: Questions make demands on respondents. Or, to put it another way, when someone asks a question, they expect an answer.

This is obvious. But consider how much of our speech doesn't work in this way. And consider also the way in which questions compel people to give an answer. If someone asks us a question we would generally (though not always) find it rude to give no answer. There is a game at work. A social game.

When we are in the classroom, we use questions because we know they provoke answers. We also know that there is a social game that we might call the 'question-answering' game. It works like this. You ask a question and your learner gives an answer. You then ask another question and your learner gives a different answer.

You know the rules of the game, and so does your learner.

A couple of really important points follow.

First, the most influential part of the game, from our perspective, is the questions we ask. It is our questions which provoke learner thinking. Our questions which set the parameters of the game. We can use questions to open up thinking or close it down. Generally, opening up is better.

Second, your learners might know the rules of the game but refuse to follow them. Or they might try to circumvent them. For example, they might say 'I don't know', refuse to answer, or give an answer you know isn't their best.

In this book we will pursue both these points. Both sides of the question-answering game. How to ask great questions and how to elicit great responses.

We'll now think a little bit more about the first point. In what different ways do questions provoke thinking? And how can we demonstrate that they have a big influence on learners' thinking?

Let's go back to the questions from above. We'll take these two to start with:

5) How many people do you know?

6) How many people do you really know?

These questions are very similar, but they make subtly different demands, provoke subtly different types of response.

The first question is a closed question. It implies that you should give a number as an answer. The second question is more open. By including the word 'really' we are asking how many people you know well. How many people you could really say you know, in a fairly deep and meaningful sense.

Simply by inserting a single word into the question, we have changed the kind of thinking it is likely to provoke. And, as a consequence, the kind of answers we're likely to get once we ask it.

Here are another pair of questions from above:

7) Where do you think learning happens?

8) Can you define learning?

The second question is highly directive. It could be answered with a yes or a no, but it's more likely that you would answer by saying 'yes' and then following up with a definition. The first question is a little more ambiguous. It is open-ended. The subject is defined, but there is not much more to go on. The person answering must decide how they are going to answer. What they're going to think about and how they might translate that into words.

The second question is not really ambiguous at all. It is also a familiar type of question. We are often asked to define things. Particularly when we are in school. This type of question cues up our previous experiences of how to answer. The first question, on the other hand, is somewhat different and less familiar. Again, we have to do more thinking, and more space is left in which we can explore possible answers.

Finally, let us look at one more of the questions:

4) What if you had a different hat you could wear?

This question has an interesting question stem. A question stem is the first bit of a question. The bit that starts things off. Here, the question stem is 'What if...'

Starting questions with 'What if...' means posing a hypothetical situation. It means we are asking learners to speculate, reason and think creatively. In this particular example, we are setting up a situation in which there is an existing reality (the one in which you are wearing your favourite hat) and a range of possible alternative realities (the ones in which you are wearing a different hat). The question asks us to think creatively about what could be, rather than what currently is.

Seen together, these different examples illustrate the way in which questions have the capacity to influence learners' thinking. It follows that we should pay attention to the questions we use with our learners. We should think critically about them and be aware that they have a significant role to play in the classroom.

A great attitude to adopt, one that will benefit the learners you work with, is to think about your questions before you ask them and after you've asked them. Before you pose a question, ask yourself whether it is likely to close down thinking or open it up. And after you've asked a question, ask yourself whether it got the response you were expecting.

Thinking in this way helps you to be more critical about your questioning. Over time, it will help you to refine and improve the quality of your questions.

Learners tend to get used to the kinds of questions we pose. They know what to expect. This has advantages and disadvantages. On the one hand, it can make it easier for the learner to interpret your questions, give appropriate responses and share their thinking. On the other hand, it might make life a little too easy for your learners. If they know what to expect they might not do as much thinking as they would otherwise do. And they might be ready to answer your questions before you ask them.

Another nice technique to adopt is making a conscious effort to vary the kinds of questions you ask. Think about using different question stems, different subjects and different types of questions. The simplest way to do this is to use a mixture of open and closed questions. Another option is to identify a range of question stems and use these as the basis for your questions. For example:

Where…

When…

Who…

How…

Why...

What...

By creating variety in your questions you create variety in learners' thinking. And by varying your questions you provoke different kinds of thinking.

In the remainder of this book we'll look at a whole host of questioning strategies and techniques you can use to support and develop your learners. Some will focus on provoking thinking – on the types of questions you ask – and some will focus on eliciting responses – how to get good answers from your learners. All are easy to use, ready to go and adaptable.

My last piece of advice is to read on, see what you like the look of and give it a go in lessons. See what the results are and see which questioning techniques work for you and your learners. Good results are sure to follow.

Summary

Questions provoke thinking. They make demands on learners. When we ask a question, we play a social game. The most important rule of this game is that questions need answers.

We use questions to help learners think. The kind of questions we ask have a big impact on the kind of thinking learners do. Paying close attention to your questioning means paying close attention to the kind of thinking you want to stimulate in the minds of your learners.

Varying your questioning means varying the kind of thinking you are asking learners to do. Thinking critically about your questioning means giving yourself and your learners the best chance for successful and stimulating interactions. This helps learners to learn more and to make better progress.

In the rest of the book we look at techniques you can use to ask great questions as well as strategies you can use to get great responses from your learners.

Chapter 2 – Opening Up Learner Thinking

We want to use questioning to open up learner thinking, rather than close it down. Here's an example of the difference:

Learner: I'm not sure...

Teaching Assistant: This is the right way, isn't it? Do you remember?

Learner: Yeah, OK.

Learner: I'm not sure...

Teaching Assistant: Can you remember doing something like this before? What might help you?

Learner: Well, maybe it's a bit like what we were doing on Monday...

In the first example, the teaching assistant tries to do too much too soon. The questions are used with good intentions, but they close down the learner's thinking. They do the work for the learner, leaving them with little to do but agree.

In the second example, the teaching assistant uses their questioning to help the learner to be independent. They consciously avoid doing too much too soon, encouraging the learner to use their own knowledge and understanding to find an answer.

When we're questioning learners, there are a couple of rules of thumb we can have in mind to help us:

i) Use questions to open up thinking

ii) Avoid doing too much work for the learner

This goes back to the points we made in the first chapter. Questions provoke thinking and encourage responses. The kind of questions we ask influence the kind of thinking and the kind of responses we get from learners. Keeping the two rules in mind helps avoid situations like the first example and increases the likelihood of situations similar to the second.

With that in mind, let's look at five techniques we can use to open up learner thinking.

1) Might – Making Knowledge Provisional

Consider the difference between these two questions:

- What is democracy?

- What might democracy be?

The second question is much more open than the first. We have achieved this by including the word 'might'. The word makes knowledge provisional. It signals to the learner that we are not looking for a definite answer. Not yet, anyway. Instead, we are implying that there are lots of possible answers out there. We want the learner to suggest one, and we can then go from there. It opens up the discussion in a way that is not so evident in the first question.

'What is democracy?' implies that we want a definite answer. There is a definition of democracy out there and we want the learner to give it to us. Now, this question might be appropriate further down the line, when we want to check learner knowledge, but earlier on in the learning cycle it might actually discourage a learner from answering.

They might feel the question implies the need for a correct answer. And if they don't know what that is, or if they are uncertain about it, they might simply guess, or give no answer at all.

Including the word 'might' subtly shifts the emphasis of your questions. It subtly changes the rules of the game. Learners often feel emboldened by this and happier to have a go.

Here are some other examples to illustrate the difference:

- 'What is the answer?' becomes 'What might the answer be?'

- 'How can we prove that?' becomes 'How might we try to prove that?'

- 'Why did the Vikings invade Britain?' becomes 'Why might the Vikings have invaded Britain?'

Using 'might' in your questions opens learning up and gives learners more scope to think about their answers. Try it out and see what difference it makes to your interactions with learners.

2) Reframe Your Questions

Sometimes we ask a question and find ourselves disappointed by the answers we receive. Maybe they are shorter, simpler or less relevant than we expected. Maybe we feel like our questioning has closed learning down – without us intending this to happen. Or without us realising that it could happen.

For example, a teaching assistant might unwittingly fall into the trap of asking a series of closed questions to a learner during a literacy lesson. After a few minutes they notice that they are doing most of the work. The learner is not thinking as much as they could do.

At this point, all is not lost! Once you are thinking more critically about your questioning, you will start to notice when these types of situation develop. And when you do spot this is happening, that is a perfect point at which to stop, have a think and reframe your questions.

Reframing is where we take the question we have asked, change it, and then ask it again to our learners. Here's an example:

Teaching Assistant: What's the answer to this one?

Learner: Um, I'm not sure…

Teaching Assistant: OK, let's think about it another way. How did we try to find out the answer last time? Do you think we could do the same thing here?

In this example, the learner is uncertain. Perhaps they lack confidence. As a result, they do not feel like they can give an answer to the initial question. The teaching assistant hears the learner's response and uses this as a cue to think critically about the question they asked.

On reflection, they wonder if it is their question which has led to the learner responding in this way. This is very different from taking the learner's response at face value and assuming they don't know the answer or are not in a position to provide an answer of some sort.

The teaching assistant reframes their question. They ask it in a different way. And they even let the learner know that they are doing this. The reframed questions open learning up and give the learner more opportunity to share their thinking and call on their previous experience to provide an answer.

3) Dig Deeper with a Second Question

Sometimes learners see the question-answer game as something they need to play because that is what you do in the classroom. They don't necessarily see the value of thinking in depth about the questions you ask them. So, for example, they might give deliberately simple or brief responses to your questions, in the hope that this will satisfy you enough to move things on.

Here's an example:

Teaching Assistant: How might Henry have felt when he became king?

Learner: Happy.

Teaching Assistant: What do you think he wanted to do while he was king?

In this exchange, the learner offers a simple answer. They have basically fulfilled their role in the game. A question has been asked and an answer provided. But is this really what the teaching assistant was hoping to achieve? Actually, they wanted to get more from their learner. More thinking and more interaction. Compare the above with this alternative example:

Teaching Assistant: How might Henry have felt when he became king?

Learner: Happy.

Teaching Assistant: Interesting. Why do you think happy? What makes you say that?

In this example, the teaching assistant is viewing the learner's response as a starting point, rather than an end point. In the first exchange, they moved onto a new question immediately after the learner had given their answer. In the second exchange, the teaching assistant thinks about what the learner has said and poses a couple of questions they feel will open the learning up, by encouraging the learner to think again about their response.

Digging deeper with a second question means taking the first response a learner gives you as a starting point and using further questioning to open learning up, moving it in a different direction.

4) Follow Up with an 'Else' Question

What else might she have thought?

How else could we have found the right answer?

Where else might the Romans have built their fort?

Why else might it be good to share?

Who else might have benefited from the plan?

The word 'else' is central to all these questions. It signals to the learner that we want more. That their first answer was a starting point and now it is time to develop things further.

Following up with an 'else' question means pushing learners to think beyond their first thoughts. It opens learning up by encouraging learners to think about a range of possible answers. This stops them settling for a single answer or, more likely, from feeling like the first answer they give is sufficient (and represents all the thinking they need to do).

Here are a few examples of the technique in action:

Teaching Assistant: What do you think about the picture?

Learner: I like the way the colours come together.

Teaching Assistant: What else do you like about it?

Teaching Assistant: How did the battle end?

Learner: It ended when Harold was hit in the eye by an arrow.

Teaching Assistant: What else might have happened near the end?

Teaching Assistant: Why did Macbeth do what he did?

Learner: Because Lady Macbeth had a lot of power over him.

Teaching Assistant: Why else might he have done what he did?

There is nothing hugely complex going on here. But in each example, we see the teaching assistant opening up learning by focussing the learner's mind on the idea that there are other possible answers out there which might be worth exploring. This helps broaden and deepen learner understanding. And it stops them assuming that giving an answer means the end of the question-answer game.

5) Ask for Examples

As soon as you start asking for examples, you're pushing learners to go beyond their first thoughts. You probably do this already. It is a natural questioning technique to use when working with learners in the classroom:

Teaching Assistant: What habitat might that be?

Learner: I think it's a woodland.

Teaching Assistant: Can you think of any other examples of woodlands?

The follow-up question directs the learner to keep thinking about the topic. It encourages them to open up their thinking by asking them for further examples which connect to their initial thoughts.

Asking for examples brings a number of benefits. First, it gives our interaction with the learner greater depth and breadth. Second, it lets us check to see if the learner's understanding is at the level we think it is. The kind of examples they give help us to assess how well they understand what they're talking about. Third, if we consistently ask for examples then we habituate learners into giving examples. This opens up their thinking over the longer term because they get into the rhythm of developing their answers by giving examples. And all of these are good things to bring about when we're working in the classroom.

Summary

We want to use questioning to open up learning as much as possible. We want to avoid falling into the trap of closing down thinking, which can sometimes happen if we don't pay attention to the questions we are using.

When we're questioning learners, two good rules of thumb are:

i) Use questions to open up thinking

ii) Avoid doing too much work for the learner

Keeping these in mind really helps you to raise the quality of your questions and the quality of the interactions you have with your learners.

Five specific ways you can open up learning are by:

1) Using the Word 'Might'

2) Reframing Your Questions

3) Digging Deeper with a Second Question

4) Following Up with an 'Else' Question

5) Asking for Examples

Chapter 3 – Getting Past 'I Don't Know'

Many, if not all, learners will use the phrase 'I don't know' during their school careers. There is nothing wrong with this phrase. If you don't know something, it's right to say so. This can help you to learn and it avoids the situation where you pretend you know something even though you actually don't. And that's not a good situation to get into.

However, many learners may also use 'I don't know' as a get out card. They say it in an attempt to avoid the question-answer game. They say it to through you off. Or they say it as a way to try and stop you questioning them. 'I don't know' often signals a lack of confidence in a learner, an unwillingness to share ideas, or a fear of failure.

Questioning is much more effective if it generates responses other than 'I don't know'. With that in mind, here are five techniques you can use to get past that phrase and into something more interesting – something involving a lot more learning.

1) Midwife Questioning

Socrates was an Ancient Greek philosopher. He spent a lot of time asking people questions – as can be seen in the books of Plato, his pupil, where Socrates is the main character. It has been suggested that Socrates asked roughly four types of question: gadfly, midwife, stingray and ignoramus. Three feature in this book. Here we're thinking about midwife questioning.

Midwives help someone give birth. Midwife questioning helps learners give birth to ideas. When we take on the role of midwife, our aim is to use questions to draw knowledge and understanding out of learners. We want to help them articulate and verbalise their thoughts. Midwife questioning often involves us being patient. We don't expect learners to deliver their answers in full, straight away. Instead, we take time to probe and support their thinking.

For example, a teaching assistant might be working one-to-one with a learner in a literacy lesson focussed on analysing poems. The learner lacks confidence and is reluctant to share their thoughts about the poem being analysed. To hide this fact, they simply say 'I don't know' when the teaching assistant poses them a question.

The teaching assistant has a good relationship with the learner. They know their background and have an idea of why they are responding in this way. To help improve matters, they decide to play the role of midwife and use midwife questioning to help the learner get their ideas out in the open. They use questions like:

- What are some of the things someone could think about this poem?

- Can you tell me how you felt when you first heard the poem?

- What else can you tell me?

- What do you remember from the last time we analysed a poem?

- How could we talk about the poem if we were explaining it to someone else?

Notice how all of these questions are designed to support the learner verbalise their thoughts. They encourage the learner to start articulating an answer linked to the wider task of analysing the poem. Playing the role of midwife over a period of 3-5 minutes, using questions like the ones above, can help you to take a learner from 'I don't know' to a much more developed and detailed response.

2) Scrap Paper

Working memory is limited to roughly seven pieces of information, plus or minus two. This is the memory we use to process information in the moment. If you ask a learner a question, they might recall something from their long-term memory, or they might think of an answer using their working memory.

For example, we might have a learner who has memorised their twelve times table. They know it off-by-heart. If we ask them: 'What is 12 x 9?' they can retrieve the answer (108) from their long-term memory, without having to really think about. This is the advantage of learning things off-by-heart.

On the other hand, we might ask the same learner a question to which they don't yet know the answer. For example, we might say: 'What is the best way to measure the area of a room?' Here, the learner has to think about how they will answer the question. They use their working memory to do this. As there is no memorised answer stored in their long-term memory, they cannot simply provide an instant recollection.

When learners are using their working memory, they may well come up against its limits. But very often they do not realise that this is happening. In our example, the learner might start thinking about how to measure the area of a room, and quickly find themselves overloaded. As a result, they answer: 'I don't know.'

The simplest and most effective way to overcome the limitations of working memory is to use scrap paper. This helps us extend our working memory. As soon as we write information down, we are taking it out of our minds, fixing it in time and space (on the paper), and freeing up space in our working memory.

Encouraging learners to use scrap paper means encouraging them to overcome the limitations of their working memory. This makes it less likely they will say 'I don't know' and more likely they will be able to engage with your questions.

3) Prompting

Prompting is where we give learners subtle support intended to direct their attention towards something that will help them to answer. We are trying to help our learners without doing too much of the work for them. Here are some examples of prompts:

- What did we say last lesson about these types of questions?

- Didn't we have a similar question yesterday morning?

- Is that something you could use in your answer?

- Do you think the word bank might help?

- How did you start your answer last time?

In each of these examples, the teaching assistant is prompting the learner to think about something which will help them to come up with an answer. The subtlety of the prompt means the learner is still expected to do the main part of the thinking themselves. It's not a case of the teaching assistant giving the learner the answer. It's about the teaching assistant prompting the learner to think in a certain way, or about a certain thing, so they can provide an answer themselves.

You can use prompting whenever a learner says 'I don't know'. Think about what the learner knows, has done before, or can use in the present situation, and prompt them to refer to this. Sometimes learners say 'I don't know' as an almost automatic response to certain types of question. Prompting means you are helping them to step out of this routine and think more carefully about what they already know or can do, and how this might be marshalled to answer the question.

Finally, it is worth remembering that prompting is subtle. If a learner does not pick up on the signals you are sending through your prompting, don't be afraid to draw attention to what you are doing. The aim with prompting is to maintain learner independence by not doing too much of the work for them. However, you can always do a little bit more if your first attempts at prompting don't have the desired effect.

4) What if you did know?

This technique is a little tricksy, but it does sometimes work:

Teaching Assistant: How could we start our book report?

Learner: I don't know.

Teaching Assistant: What if you did know? What might you say then?

It can look a bit unlikely when written down! And it can feel a bit like that as well when you say it aloud. However, the technique has a degree of insight at its core. Let me explain.

Sometimes, when a learner says 'I don't know' they are falling into a routine with which they are familiar. Maybe they say this phrase on a regular basis, lesson after lesson. It becomes a stock response – something they say without even thinking.

Sometimes, when learners use 'I don't know' they are covering up a lack of confidence, or a degree of uncertainty over how to answer. In these situations, 'I don't know' is like a get out card the learner is playing. By saying it, they hope to extricate themselves from the question-answering game. They want to be told the correct answer, not to have to discuss their ideas with you.

In both these cases, 'I don't know' is a signal you can identify and decode. When you hear it, you can ask yourself whether it is a sign your learners are falling into old habits, or perhaps lack the confidence to give you an answer.

You are then in a position to recognise this signal, let your learners know that you recognise and accept it (so as to not deny their voice), but then push them to go beyond it: 'What if you did know? What might you say then?'

5) What would we need to know?

This technique has two parts to it. First, we show the learner that we and they are on the same team. Second, we give them a way to think positively and constructively about how to come up with an answer. Here is what it looks like in practice:

Teaching Assistant: How could we start our book report?

Learner: I don't know.

Teaching Assistant: That's OK, you don't know yet. Right, what would we need to know to come up with a good answer?

In this example, the teaching assistant acknowledges that the learner doesn't currently have an answer. By using the word 'yet' they imply that the learner will be able to give an answer in the future. They then invite the learner into a team by using the word 'we'. This implies that the teaching assistant and the learner are working together to solve this particular problem. Finally, the teaching assistant signals to the learner that there is a positive way they can both think about the problem. Instead of trying to answer the original question, the teaching assistant asks the learner to think about what they would need to know in order to come up with a good answer.

The technique redirects the learner's attention. They are encouraged to think about how they can build a path towards an answer. This is a more effective strategy than either fixating on the question to the point of frustration or trying to step out of the question-answering game by using the phrase 'I don't know.'

Summary

Helping learners get past 'I don't know' is about using techniques which subtly alter the way the question-answering game is played. You can make learners aware of what you are doing, or you can do it without explicitly informing them. Either way, you are starting from the premise that your role in the interaction between yourself and your learners is partly about facilitating their responses to your questions. Getting past 'I don't know' means getting past a roadblock to good thinking and better learning.

Five techniques you can use to achieve this are:

1) Using Midwife Questioning

2) Encouraging Learners to use Scrap Paper

3) Prompting Learners

4) Asking: 'What if you did know?'

5) Asking: 'What would we need to know?'

Chapter 4 – How to Get Better Responses

The quality of responses any teaching assistant gets to their questions can vary considerably. This is to be expected. We ask different questions to different learners at different times about different topics. It makes sense that some responses are better than others, that some are more focussed and that some perhaps miss the point. Traditionally, we use follow-up questioning to improve the quality of responses when they are not what we want. For example, if a learner's responses are way off beam, we use further questions to draw them back to where we want them to be.

There are plenty of other techniques we can use as well. Techniques which, when used consistently, help to raise the general quality of our learners' responses. In the rest of this chapter, we'll look at five such techniques.

1) Wait Time

After you ask a question……….wait. Don't expect learners to answer straightaway. Wait time means thinking time. If a learner thinks they have to give an immediate response to your question, they will focus on that, instead of thinking about what they really want to say.

Giving wait time means giving learners a chance to think about the question you've asked them. They can gather their thoughts, put them in order, maybe refine them as well. Then, they are in a position to articulate them.

Consider the difference between being asked a question and having to give a response immediately and being asked a question and being given some time to think before you respond. It's highly likely the second response will be better than the first.

If we're asking good, thoughtful questions to our learners, then we want them to think about these. Why go to the trouble of coming up with a good question if we don't then give our learners enough time to think about what it means and how they might answer it?

If you already use wait time, that's great. Keep it up.

If you don't yet use wait time, you might want to explain to your learners what you are doing when you introduce it. Otherwise, they might wonder why all of a sudden you are leaving a gap after you pose a question!

You can tell your learners outright, or you can use a line like one of the following:

- Have a think, then share your answer with me.

- Take a moment, then tell me what you think.

- Ten seconds – have a think and then we'll discuss it.

You can add each of these lines on to the end of a question, signalling to the learner that you want them to think about the question before giving an answer.

2) Talk to a Partner

If you're working with a group of learners, a good way to increase the quality of responses is to invite your learners to discuss questions with a partner before sharing answers with you:

Teaching Assistant: Why might people choose to live in cities rather than the countryside? What reasons can you come up with? Talk to your partner, then we'll share some ideas.

In this example the teaching assistant is giving the learners a signal. They are saying that answering the question is going to be a two-step process, possibly longer. Step one is to discuss the question with a partner. Step two is to share the results of these discussions with the group.

This process gives learners a chance to verbalise their initial thoughts, practice these and refine them in response to what their partner says. It also negates a bit of the social tension which can arise when we pose a question to a group of learners. Rather than one person feeling like they've been put on the spot, all learners can quickly see that everyone is in the same boat – they're all discussing the question and this is the normal thing to be doing.

You might even like to give a specific time limit. This can create a sense of urgency motivating learners to get into their discussions right from the off. For example, you might say something like:

- '10 seconds, discuss your first thoughts with your partner. Off you go!'

- '30 seconds talking time. Discuss with your partner, then we'll share'

- '60 seconds practice. Practice your ideas with your partner. See how they develop then we'll all share.'

3) Note Down Your Thoughts

If you note down your thoughts then you remove them from your working memory. This frees up space you can then use to analyse and reflect on your thinking. As adults, many of us do this all the time. To the extent that we're often not even aware that we're doing it.

For example, you might find yourself attending a staff meeting or a lecture. Before you know it, you're making a note of things, then maybe you're turning to the person next to you, pointing at your notes and talking to them about what you've written.

Or maybe you find yourself in a discussion with your partner or a friend about something which requires a bit of planning – like a holiday or a house move. Hang on, you say, let's write some of this down. In so doing, you remove information from your working memory, store it in time and space (on the paper) and the quality of the discussion improves.

We can use this principle in the classroom. Simply invite your learners to note down their thoughts when you pose them a question. When they've done this, ask them to tell you about what they've written, or invite them to reflect on whether or not they would change their first thoughts. Once learners have something written down, fixed on the paper in front of them, it becomes easier for them to talk critically about those thoughts.

At the same time, there is a visual reference point to which you can refer. For example, you might pose a question like this:

'Tina, what do you think about how Violet behaved? Make a note of any important words which come to mind.'

When Tina has noted down those important words, you can then point to them and ask her to explain further. There is now something additional between the pair of you which supplements the discussion. You have a tool you can use to help Tina develop the quality of her thinking.

4) Can you explain it to an alien?

This is a great question to ask because it really challenges learners to think carefully about their responses. Not just what they're saying, but how they're saying it as well.

Aliens have no experience of Earth. They don't know anything about how we live, what we do, what our lives are like, what we know, what we learn in school or anything else. If you want to explain something to an alien you have to go into a really high level of detail. You have to think carefully about what they won't know and you can't rely on the same kind of shared assumptions that we have with our learners.

For example, we might be in a geography lesson working one-to-one with a learner. We ask them a question like: 'What do you think is the main reason people decide to move to the UK?' We leave some wait time and then ask the learner to share their thoughts. After they've explained what they think, we ask them: 'And how would you explain what migration means?'

Here we are taking the learner back a step, to find out how secure their understanding of the key term is. They give us their answer and it's pretty good. But we want them to develop it further – and we want to really understand how much they know. So, we pose the following question: 'Now, can you explain what migration means to an alien? Imagine I'm an alien (cue laughter!). How would you explain migration to me?'

At this point, we're challenging the learner to go beyond their initial explanation. We want them to dig deeper, provide more detail and develop a more nuanced understanding of migration for us.

As part of this, you can take on the role of alien. Ask your learners questions which an alien might ask. That is, someone (or something!) who has never lived on Earth and doesn't know the first thing about migration, let alone anything else. Not only will all this result in some better, more detailed responses, but you'll probably have a lot of fun in the process as well.

5) Ignoramus Questioning

Earlier on, we mentioned Socrates, the Ancient Greek philosopher. We said that he spent a lot of time asking people questions – as can be seen in the books of Plato, his pupil, where he is the main character. We also said that Socrates asked roughly four types of question: gadfly, midwife, stingray and ignoramus and that three feature in this book. Here we're going to think about ignoramus questioning.

This is where we take on the role of an ignoramus. Someone who has a very limited understanding of the topic under discussion. It differs from the role of alien (see above) because it is more about bouncing questions back to learners. Whereas playing the alien is about getting learners to go into the greatest level of detail possible.

Here is an example exchange in which the teaching assistant is playing the role of ignoramus:

Teaching Assistant: What do you think is the best way to start a story?

Learner: I like to start my stories with a description of the main place they're set.

Teaching Assistant: What's a description?

Learner: A description is where you explain what a place is like. You use describing words. You talk about all the things there are in that place. Like who lives there, what the houses are like and if there are any animals.

Teaching Assistant: So, a description is like a road sign?

Learner: No! A road sign just tells you the name of a place. A description tells you lots of things about a place. It helps you feel what it's like to live in that place.

Teaching Assistant: But you have to live somewhere to know what it's like, don't you?

Learner: That's why you start with a description. A good description really makes you know what a place looks like. Even if you've never been there. Like, I know what Hogwarts looks like, but I've never been there. And you can't go there because it's made up!

Teaching Assistant: So, do you describe Hogwarts at the start of your stories then?

Learner: No! Hogwarts is in Harry Potter. When you write a story, you have to come up with your own places. You can't just copy what someone else has written. In my stories I describe a new place I've imagined.

Notice how the teaching assistant is playing dumb but doing so in a very thoughtful and carefully considered way. Their questions are designed to get the learner explaining their thinking in more depth. They are bouncing the discussion back to the learner by pretending not to understand. As illustrated in the example, this is a great way to give learners space in which to develop their ideas and express themselves in more depth.

Summary

If we increase the quality of learner responses then we increase the quality of the thinking our questioning provokes. At the same time, we enhance the learning students are doing and provide more opportunities for us and them to discuss, explore and refine their ideas.

You can elicit better responses in a whole host of different ways, including the five we've looked at here:

1) Using Wait Time

2) Asking Learners to Talk to a Partner

3) Asking Learners to Note Down Their Thoughts

4) Asking: 'Can you explain it to an alien?'

5) Using Ignoramus Questioning

Chapter 5 – Scaffolding Questions

Scaffolding is where we give learners an extra bit of help to access the learning. It is not about doing the work for the learner, but about doing a little bit for them, just enough so that they can engage with the work and experience success as they do.

A good rule of thumb to use when scaffolding is: 'Give the least amount of help first'. Following this rule means you avoid doing too much for your learners too soon. You help them to access the work, but you don't take away their independence.

When it comes to scaffolding questions, our aim is to find techniques we can use to make our questions just that little bit simpler, increasing the possibility that learners can engage with them. Scaffolding is best used if a learner is struggling to access the work. In our case, scaffolding is best used if a learner is struggling to access your questions, or the questions of the teacher. Here are five techniques you can use to scaffold questions and so help learners to engage with them:

1) Sub-Questions

If a learner is finding a particular question really difficult, we can scaffold that question for them by dividing it into a series of sub-questions. For example, we might ask the following question to a learner with whom we are working one-to-one in a design and technology lesson:

'In what situations is it best to use a tenon saw?'

Our learner finds design and technology difficult. They lack confidence and struggle to give an answer. To make life a little easier, to scaffold the question for them, we subdivide it into three simpler questions, which we then ask in turn:

'What is a tenon saw like?'

'What other types of saw have we learned about?'

'When do you think a tenon saw is most useful?'

These questions help the learner answer the original question. They take the learner on a short journey. Each step of that journey involves the learner doing some of the thinking required to answer our original question.

Individually, the questions are simpler than our starting point of 'In what situations is it best to use a tenon saw?' This is where the scaffolding happens. We are taking the learner away from the bigger, complex question, and giving them a means to access it – through answering the three simpler questions.

You can use this technique in most situations. It tends to be most useful when learners find themselves up against a complex or challenging question.

2) Answer Options

If a learner is finding it hard to come up with an answer to a question, you can help them out by providing a range of answers from which to select. Giving a set of answer options means scaffolding a learner's interaction with a question. Here's an example of what it might look like:

Teaching Assistant: Should the three bears punish Goldilocks for eating their porridge?

Learner: Um, I'm not sure. What do you think?

Teaching Assistant: OK, well let's try it a different way. Do you think the bears should tell Goldilocks off? Do you think they should let Goldilocks go without saying anything? Or, do you think the bears should call the fairy-tale police?

In this example, the learner is uncertain about their answer. They seek help from the teaching assistant by asking them what they think. This signals their interest in the question, but also their uncertainty over how to come up with a response.

The teaching assistant chooses not to directly answer the learner's question. This is a good move at this point. To do so would close learning down when what we really want is to open it up. The learner wants the teaching assistant to tell them the answer. The teaching assistant wants to get the learner thinking, wants to help them access the learning and wants them to be as independent as possible.

Providing a set of three answer options means the teaching assistant is scaffolding the original question. They are giving the learner a little bit of support, but not too much. They are doing some of the work for the learner, but then expecting them to take the lead from this point forwards.

In this case, the teaching assistant has sketched out the three main positions the learner could take when answering the question. It is now up to the learner to decide which one they agree with. And a discussion between the learner and the teaching assistant can progress from there.

3) Continuum

Draw a line on a piece of paper. Put a couple of smaller lines at each end so it becomes a double-ended arrow, pointing in two directions at once. Write 'Strongly Agree' under the left-hand side arrow. Write 'Strongly Disagree' under the right-hand side arrow. You now have a continuum.

This is a great scaffolding tool. Learners can use it to think about questions. It provides a space within which they can place their answers. And it achieves this without doing too much of the work for them. In fact, it does very little of the work. Just enough to make life a bit easier. Just enough to give learners a way into the question.

Let's look at an example:

Teaching Assistant: Do you think it would have been good to live in Ancient Egypt?

Learner: Um...maybe. I'm not sure. There's a lot to think about.

Teaching Assistant: OK, let's draw a continuum [teaching assistant draws a double-ended arrow, labels the ends 'Strongly Agree' and 'Strongly Disagree']. Right, have a look at the continuum. Now, do you think Ancient Egypt was a good place to live? Where would you place yourself on the line?

By drawing the continuum, the teaching assistant gives the learner something concrete they can grab hold of. They no longer need to think about all the possible answers they could give to the initial question. It is something slightly different they now need to do. They need to place themselves on the continuum. To answer the question, they need to look at the line and decide where they would put themselves.

A continuum scaffolds learning by setting out the range of possible answers. Learners are then invited to select their answer by placing themselves at an appropriate point on the continuum. When they have done this, the teaching assistant can ask them about their choice. A discussion ensues during which the learner and the teaching assistant can talk about the question at length.

One important point to note. Let your learners know that they can change their position on the continuum later on, if they wish. This ensures they don't see their first answer as binding. It lets them change their minds if they begin to feel differently as the discussion develops.

4) Place Your Token

This technique takes some elements of 'Answer Options' and 'Continuum'. It is a variation, giving you another way in which to scaffold learner answers. Here's how it works:

The teaching assistant poses a question to their learner. They then write down three or four possible answers. The learner is given a token, and the teaching assistant says: 'Which do you think is the best answer? Where would you like to place your token?' The learner thinks about the question, looks at the possible answers written out by the teaching assistant and places their token on the answer they think is best. A discussion then develops, stimulated by the choice the learner has made.

There are a couple of really nice features to this technique. First, the learner is given a sense of agency, even though they are struggling to answer the initial question and need the scaffolding the teaching assistant is providing. This sense of agency comes from the fact that the learner has the token and it is up to them where they place it.

Second, the learner is in a position to move their token later on, during the course of the discussion they have with the teaching assistant. This means that if the learner gets the answer wrong first time around, or if they change their mind, they can take control of the situation and visually demonstrate their change of heart by moving the token.

When writing out the collection of answers from which you want your learner to choose, think about the kind of answers which are most likely to stimulate a good discussion. For example, you might want to deliberately throw in a few common mistakes or misconceptions. Not in an attempt to catch your learner out, but in an effort to draw out any mistakes or misconceptions they might be labouring under.

A final point to note is that mini-whiteboards are handy for this technique. You can write your question at the top, then include three or four answers underneath, and even put boxes next to each one in which the learner can place their token.

5) Clueing

In Chapter Four we looked at 'Prompting' as a technique to help get learners past 'I don't know.' Here we can think about clueing. This is the next level on from prompting. In clueing, we give learners a bit more help and support. They are not as independent as when we prompt. Hence why the technique is included here under scaffolding. It's useful on those occasions when our learners need that extra bit of support to access the learning and to make sense of what is going on.

Here is an example of a teaching assistant using clueing to support a learner:

Teaching Assistant: How can we solve the problem the teacher has set?

Learner: Um...maybe...no, wait a minute...I'm not sure what to do.

Teaching Assistant: Do you think we could find some help on page 27 of the textbook? Didn't that have an example of a similar type of problem?

The teaching assistant is not doing all the work for the learner. They're giving them a clue directing them to a place where they can find the answer. Or, at least, where they can find information which will help them to come up with an answer.

Clueing means using questioning to send learners in certain directions. It means helping them to target their efforts in a useful way. In our example, we can see that the learner is floundering. They are thinking about the question and trying to come up with an answer, but they can't quite get there. The teaching assistant steps in to scaffold the situation, to offer their support. They do this through clueing. By using the clues contained in the teaching assistant's questions, the learner is in a position to come up with an answer – to access the learning.

Summary

When we scaffold questions, we find ways to help learners access the learning our questions provoke. We don't want to do too much of the work for our learners, but we do want to help them engage with our questions. Scaffolding is best used when learners are struggling to engage with our questions. Giving the least amount of help first means promoting learner independence and giving ourselves somewhere to go if learners still struggle to engage with our questions.

Five ways you can scaffold questions are:

1) Breaking a Question Down into Sub-Questions

2) Providing Answer Options

3) Using a Continuum

4) Using Answer Tokens

5) Clueing

Chapter 6 – Open vs Closed Questions

Open and closed questions both have their uses. Both have much to offer. As a rule, open questions are to be preferred to closed questions. Open questions have more scope. They give learners more space in which to think, explore and discuss. Closed questions tend to look for definite or singular answers. They are therefore good for checking knowledge and simulating test environments, as well as some other uses.

When working with learners on a day-to-day basis, try to focus on open questions wherever you can. These tend to open up learning, whereas closed questions may well close it down. With those thoughts in mind, here are a selection of techniques connected to open and closed questioning. The first technique combines the two, techniques two and three focus on open questioning and the last two techniques look at closed questioning.

1) From Closed to Open

If a learner is struggling to access the work, or is lacking in confidence, one way you can use questioning to support them is by coming up with a series of questions that run from closed to open. Here's an example:

Teaching Assistant: Is this a shape you've seen before?

Learner: No

Teaching Assistant: Does it look more like a square or a rectangle?

Learner: A rectangle

Teaching Assistant: Does it have four sides?

Learner: Yes

Teaching Assistant: Could we draw lines here and here so as to make two triangles and a square?

Learner: Yes

Teaching Assistant: The shape is called a parallelogram. How do you think we could try to find out its area?

The teaching assistant knows the learner has not come across parallelograms before. So, they use a series of closed questions to help the learner get comfortable with the new shape. The questions direct the learner's attention, allowing them to focus on different properties of the shape in turn.

The fifth question is an open one. It invites the learner to think a bit more deeply than the first four questions. By this point, the teacher has primed the learner's mind with lots of key information about parallelograms. They are new to the learner, they look a bit like a rectangle, they have four sides and you can divide them up into two triangles and a square. The learner now has all of this information close at hand – close in their memory. They can use it to help them answer the fifth question. The open one.

The exchange illustrates how you can use a series of closed questions to prepare the groundwork for an open question. It's about taking learners on a short journey which gets them into a good position from which to think more deeply. That is, a position from which they are well-placed to answer an open question.

2) Big Picture Questions

Thinking about the big picture helps learners place their learning in context. It also gives meaning to learning, helping children to understand why they are doing what they are doing and how it connects to the wider world, as well as to their own lives.

Big picture questions are nearly always open. This is because they ask learners to think about their learning from a wider, broader perspective than what they might be used to. You can use them to help learners feel more engaged with a topic, to make connections between different areas of their learning, and to make sense of what they are studying and why it matters. Here are some examples of big picture questions:

- Who might use trigonometry in their work? What jobs might use trigonometry on a daily basis?

- Why might society think it's important we learn about persuasive writing?

- How many different situations can you think of where it might be helpful to know about the history of Britain?

- How might the Romans have influenced our lives today? What traces of their presence can you think of?

- How could we use the lessons of Goldilocks to help us in our daily lives?

In each example, the teaching assistant is using the question to broaden out learner thinking. The questions are big and open-ended. They invite learners to think about the wider world and their wider knowledge – to connect this to the current topic of study. Asking questions like this means helping learners to take a step back from their learning and to see it in a wider context.

It's like the learner is looking down a microscope, so they can understand something really clearly. But we then ask them to change their point of view, so they step away from the microscope, look up and see how what they are examining fits into a bigger picture.

3) Open Questions Connected to Prior Experience

At the beginning of a topic, we want to quickly get our learners engaged in their learning. We want them to feel inspired and excited by the new topic. But, we also realise that this won't always be the case. And, a more realistic goal might be that we want our learners to be in a position to make sense of the topic, and to feel like they can throw themselves into and be successful.

One of the best ways to quickly achieve this goal is to focus our questioning on learners' prior knowledge. Our aim is to draw their existing knowledge and understanding into the open, so that we can gain a good idea of where they are at, and so that our learners feel they are meeting the new topic with an existing level of skill and experience.

There are very few topics on the curriculum where learners arrive without any past experience on which they might call – even if that past experience is tangential rather than directly connected.

Open questions are most relevant because they give learners plenty of scope to think about what they know and to connect this to the new topics. Closed questions can sometimes be useful in these situations, but not always. Plus, to effectively use closed questions to elicit prior knowledge often takes a bit longer (as you have to try different avenues to build up a general picture of what learners know and understand, whereas open questions naturally lend themselves to learners sharing more information more quickly).

With those thoughts in mind, here are some examples of open questions connected to prior experience you can use at the start of a topic:

- What do you already know about this?

- How many words can you tell me that connect to this topic?

- What other topics might this connect to?

- Where have we seen these keywords before? What can you think of?

- How does this link to what you already know?

In each case, the question gives learners a chance to share their prior knowledge. In so doing, they make the teaching assistant aware of what they already know and make themselves aware of this as well. In the latter case, this primes them to engage with the new topic and to make use of their existing experience as they do so.

4) Closed Questions for Checking Knowledge

One of the best uses of closed questions is for checking knowledge. This is important throughout the teaching cycle. At the start of a new topic, we want to check what learners know about the topic, as well as what they remember from previous topics. During the teaching phase, we want to check that they are remembering the things they are learning. And we want to check whether they are learning information correctly. For example, are they remembering things accurately, or are they making mistakes or remembering misconceptions?

Finally, we want to check knowledge at the end of the teaching cycle. This lets us see how much learners have learned, how much they can remember and what information they have retained.

Closed questions are useful for checking knowledge quickly, for focussing in on recall, and for targeting a specific area of a child's learning. For example, at the end of a topic looking at forces in science, we might use a series of closed questions to check what learners can remember about forces.

Or, halfway through a topic looking at coastal erosion, we might use a series of closed questions to check whether or not learners have memorised the keywords and key ideas they need to know to be successful in the remaining lessons.

When using closed questions to check knowledge, remember that the point is not just to identify what learners know and what they don't know. It is also to then use this information to intervene effectively. For example, if the teaching assistant in our imaginary geography lessons identifies that their learners are struggling with the difference between abrasion and attrition, then they can use this information to reteach the difference. The information our closed questions elicit thus informs future interaction. It is both evidence of what the learner knows and suggestive of what the teaching assistant should do next, in response.

5) Closed Questions for Practice Testing

Practice testing is one of the most effective techniques we can use to help learners improve their recall of information. It is any situation in which we recreate exam-style conditions to test our learners on the things they know. The important thing to remember is that practice testing should always be low-stakes. It is about improving recall, rather than trying to get everything right. If learners feel the stakes are high, then they are less likely to stay engaged, to put in their best effort and to have a go without fearing what might happen if they get something wrong.

You don't have to use closed questions for practice testing, but they do work well. Here's an example set of practice testing questions a teaching assistant might use to help a learner improve their recall of information:

1) What is the definition of democracy?

2) How many MPs sit in the House of Commons?

3) What stops the government doing whatever it wants?

4) Can you name three select committees?

5) Who was prime minister before Tony Blair?

6) What date was Magna Carta?

7) What is royal assent?

8) What is a 'vote of no confidence'?

9) What does the chancellor of the exchequer do?

10) Where does the prime minister live?

The teaching assistant can use these questions to test the learner's recall of key information. They can do this verbally, or by creating a set of flashcards with the questions written on one side and the answers written on the other.

An advantage of using closed questions in this way is that you can repeat the practice testing (giving learners the opportunity to practice recalling the information and to improve on any mistakes or errors) and you can also pick up the pace, asking the questions increasingly quickly as you repeat them.

For example, our teaching assistant might use the set of ten questions outlined above to test their learner by posing them five times, speeding up on each occasion, challenging the learner to recall the information more quickly, and to correct any mistakes made as they go.

Summary

Both open and closed questions have their benefits. Both are useful, though in different ways and at different times. Open questions are to be preferred as a general rule of thumb because they promote discussion, exploration and engagement with ideas and topics. Try to use open questions as much as possible when you are working with learners. They open learning up and help learners to develop their thinking in more depth and detail. Closed questions tend to be useful at specific times and for specific purposes.

Here are five techniques, linked to open and closed questioning, you can use in the classroom:

1) Use a series of closed questions to build up to an open question

2) Use Big Picture Open Questions

3) Use Open Questions Connected to Prior Knowledge

4) Use Closed Questions to Check Knowledge

5) Use Closed Questions for Practice Testing

Chapter 7 – Creative Questioning Techniques

The potential for thinking creatively with and through questioning is limitless. Questions provoke thinking therefore they have the potential to provoke creative thinking. We can make anything the subject of our questions and, through this, we have the opportunity to ask creative questions, to question creatively and to provoke creative thinking in our learners.

Here are five techniques you can use, all of which bring a creative element to the act of questioning.

1) What If... Questions

'What if...' questions really challenge learners to think creatively. They set out a hypothetical situation which shapes learner responses. They need to speculate, reason and think creatively to provide an answer. Here are some examples:

- What if you could live in Roman Britain? What might it be like?

- What if you could speak to Hansel and Gretel? What would you tell them?

- What if World War Two had ended three years earlier?

- What if space travel was as cheap and easy as train travel?

- What if ducks could talk? What might they say?

In each of these example, 'What if...' is used to set up an unusual situation, stimulating learners to think in ways they might otherwise have ignored or struggled to access. We can use 'What if...' questions to help learners change their thinking. They help learners to think about the topics they are studying from different angles, at the same time as they stimulate creative thinking.

When using 'What if...' questions, you might like to give your learners some examples of how they could answer or the kind of things they could think about in their answers. This gives learners a little scaffolding they can use to engage with the questions, if they are having difficulty in doing so.

Another interesting option when it comes to 'What if...' questions is to turn the tables and invite your learners to come up with their own. Here, the idea is to give learners experience of developing questions and thinking creatively by giving them the question stem 'What if...' along with some examples, and then inviting them to come up with the most interesting questions they can think of. You and they can then work together to try to answer these questions.

2) Stingray Questions

We now come to our third example of Socratic questioning. We've already looked at midwife and ignoramus questioning – two of the techniques employed by the Ancient Greek philosopher Socrates. Now we'll take a look at stingray questioning, another one of his approaches.

Stingray questions pack a jolt. Like the sting of a stingray. They shock or surprise learners, causing them to look at things from a different perspective. Stingray questions might shake learning up, turn it on its head, or challenge learners to think differently about what they thought they knew. There is some overlap between stingray questions and 'What if...' questions. A stingray question might begin with 'What if...' but they also come in lots of other forms as well. Here are some examples:

- Would gravity still work if the Earth was the same size as the moon?

- If Goldilocks was able to get into the bears' house, isn't it their fault for not being more security conscious?

- What might a world be like where maps had never been invented?

- Why can't other animals talk?

- How might history be different if no one had ever written anything down?

In each of these examples, the teaching assistant's aim is to get their learners thinking critically and creatively. The stingray questions take normal thinking, or the thinking with which learners are familiar, and deliberately try to undermine it.

This isn't done with the intention of putting learners off. The aim is to get them thinking differently. And to get them looking more closely at what they thought they knew.

For example, the third question, 'What might a world be like where maps had never been invented?' encourages the learner to think about their existing knowledge of maps, and then imagine a world where this knowledge was irrelevant. They have to look at the idea of maps, the way maps are used, and the consequences of maps existing, and use this to think creatively – to reason and speculate – about a world where maps have never existed.

For these reasons, stingray questions are particularly useful when learners have developed a secure knowledge of a topic, or for when you want to jolt them out of their familiar ways of thinking. And, of course, they are also a lot of fun!

3) If this is the answer, what might the question be?

For example:

Teaching Assistant: Cells. If this is the answer, what might the question be?

Learner: [Thinks about it, makes a couple of notes] Maybe, what is the human body made up of?

Teaching Assistant: Nice question – what made you go for that one?

In this technique, the question-answer game is inverted. In the usual run of things, the teacher or teaching assistant poses the question and the learner gives an answer. Here, that is turned around. The teacher or teaching assistant gives an answer and the learner must pose a question for which the answer is an appropriate response.

The technique has a number of benefits. First, it gives learners an opportunity to develop their own questions and to think about the process of question development. Second, it creates variety and engagement by deliberately inverting the rules of the game the learner and teaching assistant are used to. Three, it opens up possibilities for creative thinking because the learner has to think backwards – in an unfamiliar way. They take the answer they are given and use it as starting point. Whereas the usual practice is to be given a question and to use that as your starting point.

You can use the technique to stretch and challenge your learners, to test their knowledge, and to give them a break from the usual routine.

Another option worth considering is that you can extend the technique. Returning to our example above, the teaching assistant might take a response from their learner and then say the following: 'OK, now can you come up with another question for which 'cells' could be the answer? Try to make it different from your first one.'

4) Word Selection

Teaching Assistant: What might be the best way to look after the environment?

Learner: I think everybody should try to do their bit. You should recycle things at home and make sure you switch off all the lights when you're not using them.

Teaching Assistant: That's an interesting answer. How about we see if we can develop it? Can you give me another answer, this time using at least one of these words: sustainable, climate, challenges, environment and renewable?

This technique is all about encouraging learners to develop the answers they give you and to do so by including key vocabulary you know they need to be thinking about.

In the example, the learner gives an answer and the teaching assistant takes this as a starting point, not an end point. They challenge the learner to think again about their answer and to be creative. This creativity is primarily about redeveloping the original answer so it includes one or more of the key words the teaching assistant has shared.

The technique can be used in all sorts of different situations. Depending on who you are working with, you can either provide the selection of words verbally, or write them down for the learner to see. The second option is better if the learner lacks confidence or finds learning a bit trickier than some of their peers. Noting the words down means the learner does not have store them in their working memory while also trying to think about how they can develop their original answer.

A final point to note is that you can develop the technique by passing the word selection element over to your learners. This increases the level of challenge and requires even more creative thinking. Here's an example:

Teaching Assistant: What might be the best way to look after the environment?

Learner: I think everybody should try to do their bit. You should recycle things at home and make sure you switch off all the lights when you're not using them.

Teaching Assistant: That's an interesting answer. How about we see if we can develop it? Can you suggest five different words connected to the topic we could include in a new answer?

Learner: [Thinks about the question] How about wildlife, habitat, changes, green and energy?

Teaching Assistant: That's a really nice selection – they do all connect. Now, what would an answer be like that included some of those words?

5) Question Maps

Question maps help learners visualise their thinking about a specific question. They can help them to see connections between different parts of their thinking, to think creatively, and to provide higher quality answers as well.

Imagine you are working with a group of four learners in a religious studies lesson. The teacher has posed a big question to the whole class: 'Why do people like to take part in religious festivals?' This follows on from some work the class have been doing looking at festivals in different religious traditions.

The question is a big one. It's open-ended and gives plenty of scope for discussion and exploration. You decide to use question mapping as a way to help your learners think carefully and creatively about the question. You say something like the following:

'OK, we're going to work in two pairs. Each pair gets a sheet of paper. Let's write the question in the middle of the paper, put a circle round it, and use this as our starting point. Now, I want you to make a map showing all the different things we could talk about when answering this question. Draw lines coming off the centre circle and label these with your different ideas. You can then start to connect different ideas together, add in extra lines, draw pictures, write down additional questions and so on. Anything you like! After five minutes, we'll share our maps with each other and see what we've come up with. Then we'll try to answer the question – and come up with the best answer possible.'

The technique gives learners an opportunity to fix their ideas on paper. Having done this, they can start to make connections between different ideas and can look at their thinking as a whole. The map they create provides a really useful, effective visualisation of their thinking. Something they can then share with you and their peers.

Summary

There are many ways we can use questioning to provoke creative thinking – just as there are many ways we can make our questioning more creative. When encouraging learners to be creative it is also good to model creative thinking for them. This provides something they can borrow from, imitate or copy. It gives them a starting point. If some learners struggle to get going, modelling creative thinking gives them a way in.

Five creative questioning techniques you can use in the classroom are:

1) 'What if...' Questions

2) Stingray Questions

3) If this is the answer, what might the question be?

4) Word Selection

5) Question Maps

Chapter 8 – Bloom's Taxonomy Questioning

Bloom's Taxonomy was put together in the 1950s by a group of academics in America. Benjamin Bloom chaired the committee who developed it, hence the name. The taxonomy ranks the kind of thinking learners do in school. It identifies six key types of thinking and puts these in order, from simplest to most difficult. Here is the taxonomy:

- Level 1: Knowledge

- Level 2: Comprehension

- Level 3: Application

- Level 4: Analysis

- Level 5: Synthesis

- Level 6: Evaluation

The first level is knowledge. Knowing or remembering things. This is the simplest type of thinking. The second level is comprehension. Understanding what things mean. The third level is application. Being able to apply your understanding to do things like complete tasks.

Level four is analysis. This is more complex. It is where you can start to break things down and see how they work. Level five is synthesis – another word for creation.

This is where the learner can use all their knowledge and understanding to create new things. And level six is evaluation. This is where the learner can use everything they know to make judgements. To assess and evaluate things.

You can use Bloom's Taxonomy to come up with questions to ask your learners. Choose a level of the taxonomy you think is appropriate for the situation, and then come up with a question linked to it.

For example, if a learner is really struggling with a topic, you might decide to ask them some knowledge questions. This is the simplest level and so should be accessible for the learner. If it is not, then you know they need a lot more support to get to grips with the basics of the learning.

In another example, we might find a teaching assistant working with a learner who is confident with the topic. To challenge this learner's thinking, the teaching assistant decides to go for an evaluation question, right at the top of the taxonomy. By doing this they hope to really push the learner to think deeply about their learning.

Another advantage of using Bloom's Taxonomy is that you can move up or down it in response to learner answers. So, for example, if you start out with some knowledge-based questions and discover these are too easy for your learner, you can move up a level and try some comprehension-based questions instead.

Moving up and down Bloom's Taxonomy means changing the difficulty of your questions. Or, to put it another way, it means changing the difficulty of the thinking you are asking learners to do.

But maybe this is a bit harder than it sounds. How do we know what questions look like at each of the levels? And how can we be sure the questions we ask fit the level we intend to use?

In the remainder of this chapter we'll answer these questions. Below you'll find keywords and examples for all six levels. You can use them to come up with your own questions to use with your learners:

1) Knowledge Questions

Knowledge Keywords: Arrange, Define, Describe, List, Match, Memorise, Name, Order, Quote, Recognise, Recall, Repeat, Reproduce, Restate, Retain.

This is the simplest level of understanding. We can use knowledge-based questions to help learners access the learning, to support them if they are low on confidence and to work out how much they already know about a topic.

Here are some examples of knowledge-based questions:

i) Can you match the words to the pictures?

ii) Can you put the numbers in order?

iii) Can you recognise the kings and queens of England?

iv) Can you repeat what you heard?

v) Can you write a list of all the words connected to gardening?

vi) Can you remember the definition of alliteration?

vii) Can you name three things a spaceman would need?

2) Comprehension Questions

Comprehension Keywords: Characterise, Classify, Complete, Describe, Discuss, Establish, Explain, Express, Identify, Illustrate, Recognise, Report, Relate, Sort, Translate.

This is a slightly more developed level of understanding. This is when learners can go beyond simply recalling information. They can explain ideas, describe what things mean and go into more detail. We can use comprehension-based questions to push learners' thinking, find out what they understand and encourage them to think more deeply about the topic.

Here are some examples of comprehension-based questions:

i) How would you describe Monet's style?

ii) How would you explain photosynthesis?

iii) Can you identify the most relevant sections?

iv) Can you illustrate that with an example?

v) Can you recognise the equations which will be harder to solve?

vi) How would you sort these into push factors and pull factors?

vii) Can you translate the story into a cartoon strip?

3) Application Questions

Application Keywords: Apply, Calculate, Choose, Demonstrate, Dramatize, Employ, Implement, Interpret, Operate, Perform, Practise, Role-Play, Sketch, Solve, Suggest.

This is the next level of development. This is when learners can take what they know and understand (Levels 1 and 2) and use this to do a variety of things. For example, a learner might use their knowledge and understanding of fractions to solve new problems the teacher sets them. Application is all about putting your learning to use. Applying it to a task, problem or question. Application-based questions encourage learners to do this, to make use of their knowledge and understanding.

Here are some examples of application-based questions:

i) What answers can you suggest?

ii) What do you suggest the coach should do to change things?

iii) Can you demonstrate which is the best option?

iv) Can you use your knowledge of maps to make sense of this one?

v) How would you turn this into a role-play, to show the key ideas?

vi) Can you sketch a solution to the problem?

vii) Which is the best choice for Goldilocks and why?

4) Analysis Questions

Analysis Keywords: Analyse, Appraise, Categorize, Compare, Contrast, Differentiate, Discriminate, Distinguish, Examine, Experiment, Explore, Investigate, Question, Research, Test.

This is the fourth level and represents a more sophisticated stage of learning. Learners can start to effectively analyse ideas, information, situations, problems and tasks when they are sufficiently confident with the knowledge and understanding they have developed. At this point, learners are starting to think critically. They've gone from knowing, understanding and applying to looking in detail at things – and using their knowledge, understanding and ability to do this. Analysis-based questions challenge learners to go into depth and to look at things much more carefully.

Here are some examples of analysis-based questions:

i) What are the key differences between democracy and autocracy?

ii) Can you compare and contrast France and Germany?

iii) What questions would you ask to find out more?

iv) How could you research the topic in more detail?

v) What are the main differences between the Roman Empire and the Ottoman Empire?

vi) How might you investigate whether or not what the newspaper says is true?

vii) How would you distinguish between a simple sum and a complex one?

5) Synthesis Questions

Synthesis Keywords: Combine, Compose, Construct, Create, Devise, Design, Formulate, Hypothesise, Integrate, Merge, Organise, Plan, Propose, Synthesise, Unite.

Synthesis is the fifth level. Here we are asking learners to create new things. They use the detailed and in-depth knowledge and understanding they have developed to come up with new ways of doing things, to design new approaches, or to put together different elements in a new way. For example, we might ask a learner who has been learning about habitats to propose a new habitat that might come about in the future. To do this, they will take their existing knowledge and understanding and use it to come up with something new. Something different from what they have learned about.

Here are some examples of synthesis-based questions:

i) Can you propose a different way to answer the question?

ii) What might a plan of action look like for investigating the local environment?

iii) How would you design a poster for your campaign?

iv) What might happen if you tried to reverse the process?

v) Can you compose a letter to the minister, telling them what they should do?

vi) Can you create an alternative logo for the school?

vii) How would you bring everyone in the community together?

6) Evaluation Questions

Evaluation Keywords: Appraise, Argue, Assess, Critique, Defend, Evaluate, Examine, Grade, Inspect, Judge, Justify, Rank, Rate, Review, Value.

The sixth and final level is evaluation. This level asks learners to take all their knowledge, understanding, ability and creativity and to use it to make judgements. The idea is that you are only in a position to make good judgements about things once you fully understand them. For example, imagine we have two learners. Learner A has just started studying habitats, while Learner B has been studying habitats for three weeks. If we ask them both the question 'What are the strengths and weaknesses of this habitat?' Learner B is going to provide us with a much better answer – because they can call on all the knowledge and understanding they have developed over the period.

Here are some examples of evaluation-based questions:

i) What are the pros and cons of starting again?

ii) What strengths and weaknesses can you identify?

iii) How would you justify that answer?

iv) Can you rank the sources from most to least useful?

v) Is this picture more valuable than the others? Why?

vi) What arguments can you use to support your view?

vii) Can you defend your opinion in the face of these other arguments?

Summary

Bloom's Taxonomy takes the core types of thinking learners do in the classroom and puts them in order from simplest to most complex. Each level is more challenging than the last. The six levels are:

- Level 1: Knowledge   **Simplest**

- Level 2: Comprehension

- Level 3: Application

- Level 4: Analysis

- Level 5: Synthesis

- Level 6: Evaluation   **Most Complex**

You can use Bloom's Taxonomy to come up with questions. Pick the level you think is right for your learner, then use it to develop a question. You can move up or down the taxonomy depending on the response you get.

If your first few questions are too easy, move up the taxonomy. If they are too hard, move down it. This way, you can make sure your questions are sufficiently challenging and that they meet the needs of your learners.

You can use the word banks and exemplar questions above to help you.

Chapter 9 – SOLO Taxonomy Questioning

If you're not taken by Bloom's Taxonomy, there is an alternative taxonomy you can use to structure your questions. This one is called SOLO Taxonomy. SOLO stands for Structure of Observed Learning Outcomes. It was put together in the early 1980s by Kevin Collis and John Biggs, two academics.

It works in a similar way to Bloom's Taxonomy. There are a series of levels, each more challenging than the last. SOLO Taxonomy describes the way in which learning gets more complex as it progresses. It also reflects how learners' understanding gets more complex. For example, when we start a new topic, learners don't know much about it. Their understanding is simple, maybe even basic. Therefore, the learning needs to be fairly simple to start off with.

As learners go through the topic, their understanding develops. It gets more complex. The learning grows more complex at the same time. This means learners are continually challenged, and their understanding continues to develop.

Here are the five levels of the taxonomy:

Level 1: Pre-Structural   **(Simplest)**

Level 2: Uni-Structural

Level 3: Multi-Structural

Level 4: Relational

Level 5: Extended Abstract   **(Most Complex)**

At first glance, the terms can seem a bit technical and a bit distant from the classroom. But we can quickly get past this by explaining what each level means.

Pre-Structural: This is when learners know very little about a topic – perhaps even nothing. Their understanding is basic or non-existent. There is no structure to their understanding. If they take on a task, it is not attacked appropriately; the learner doesn't really understand the point and uses too simple a way of trying to go about it. Learners are usually at this stage only at the very beginning of a topic. And many learners will arrive at a new topic knowing at least one thing about it, meaning they might miss out the pre-structural level altogether.

Uni-Structural: This is when learners know one thing about a topic. When they respond to questions or tasks, they tend to only focus on one thing. Their understanding of the topic is pretty basic. They use the one thing they know to try to make sense of questions and task. This is where learners are usually at when they start a topic. They might have some prior knowledge, or they might remember one thing about it. Keywords include: Define, Identify, State.

Multi-Structural: This is when learners know a number of things about a topic. Their understanding is developing. They've gone from knowing one thing, to knowing a few things. Maybe even quite a few. When learners try to answer questions or complete tasks, they can focus on a number of relevant things. But they do tend to see these things as independent from one another. They can't yet make connections between the different things they know. Keywords include: Describe, List, Detail, Name.

Relational: This is when learners can make connections between the different things they know. Their understanding is at a good level. It has developed and become more complex. They have gone from knowing one thing, to many things, to being able to explain how those things relate to each other. The structure of the learner's understanding has changed. It is now more like a web of connections than a list of separate items. The different things the learner has learned have become integrated into a coherent whole. When they answer questions and attempt tasks, they can call on a range of ideas and pieces of information. They know what they are trying to do and why they are trying to do it. Keywords include: Compare/Contrast, Explain, Classify, Analyse.

Extended Abstract: This is the highest level of understanding. This is when learners can connect their understanding to other areas. For example, they can see how the current topic connects to other topics they've studied. Or they can make generalisations, using the understanding they have developed. At this level, learners tend to deal confidently with questions and tasks, calling on their wide-ranging and interconnected knowledge to do so. When learners are at this level, we want to challenge them to go further – to stretch their thinking and take it to new areas. Keywords include: Evaluate, Generalise, Predict, Create, Hypothesise.

If you Google 'SOLO Taxonomy' you'll find some images showing how different pictures are used to signify these five levels. The pictures are:

Pre-Structural: A single red dot

Uni-Structural: A single yellow rectangle

Multi-Structural: Three green rectangles in a line

Relational: Three blue rectangles in a line, connected together by thinner, black lines

Extended Abstract: The same as relational, but with a diamond hanging off the top, connected by another thin, black line.

If you have time, go on Google and have a look for this.

The five pictures neatly demonstrate what the five levels mean and how understanding gets increasingly complex as you move up the levels. You can use the images as a way to memorise the five levels – and as a cue to help you recall them.

When it comes to questioning, we can use SOLO Taxonomy to help us develop questions and to assess learner responses (so as to work out their current level of understanding).

For example, you might be working one-to-one with a learner in a psychology lesson. To assess their understanding, you begin by asking some very simple, uni-structural questions. They answer these with ease so you decide to move onto multi-structural. The learner also finds these fairly easy, so you move up another level and go for some relational questions. Immediately you notice that the learner is finding it harder. Their answers are not as quick and you can see they are really having to think.

This is great! You've quickly found the right level of questioning for your learner. You know they can handle uni-structural and multi-structural questions, so you stick with the relational questions to make sure they are challenged.

Using the taxonomy in this way is similar to what we looked at with Bloom's Taxonomy. You can move up and down it in response to how learners answer your questions. This makes differentiation easy and helps you increase the quality of your interactions with learners.

Let's now look at some examples of the kind of questions you might ask at each level. These questions are generic, giving a sense of the differences between each of the levels. Feel free to use them as they are or to adapt and modify them to fit with your learners and the subjects they are learning about:

1) Level 1: Examples of Pre-Structural Questions

- What don't you understand?

- What could we learn about to know more?

- How could we start our learning?

- How will we know when we understand a good amount?

- Where do you think we should start?

2) Level 2: Examples of Uni-Structural Questions

- Can you tell me one thing about the topic?
- What is the first thing you've learned?
- What did you find out?
- What is one thing you remember?
- Can you tell me what you know?

3) Level 3: Examples of Multi-Structural Questions

- What different things do you know about the topic?
- Can you explain what that means?
- Can you give me some evidence to explain that?
- What do you think about the story?
- How many things can you remember?

4) Level 4: Examples of Relational Questions

- What similarities and differences are there?
- How do the different things fit together?
- What caused that to happen?
- What different effects did it have?

- Can you compare and contrast the two newspaper reports?

5) Level 5: Examples of Extended Abstract Questions

- What was the most influential feature?

- Can you summarise the whole thing?

- How does it connect to other topics we've studied?

- What do you predict might happen in the future?

- Do you have a hypothesis you would like to test?

The questions get more complex as we move up each level. This reflects the increasing complexity of a learner's understanding as they learn more and progress through a topic. You can move up and down the levels based on the responses you get from your learners. You can also use higher levels of the taxonomy to challenge your learners. For example, you might stretch their thinking by posing them a question from the level above where you feel they are currently at.

If you take this approach, which has much to recommend it, be aware that learners might need some extra support and scaffolding to help them answer the question effectively. Another option is to ask a higher-level question now, see how the learner does, and to then come back to that same question further down the line, after a bit more learning has taken place. You can make learners aware of what you are doing by saying something like: 'Let's see if you have a similar answer now to what you thought a couple of lessons ago.'

Summary

SOLO Taxonomy sketches out how understanding develops through a series of five levels:

Level 1: Pre-Structural   **(Simplest)**

Level 2: Uni-Structural

Level 3: Multi-Structural

Level 4: Relational

Level 5: Extended Abstract   **(Most Complex)**

These run from simplest (pre-structural) to most complex (extended abstract). We can use SOLO taxonomy to assess current levels of learner understanding and to underpin our questions. Depending where learners are at, we can pose them questions at different levels of the taxonomy, using these to engage them, challenge them and help them to develop their thinking.

Chapter 10 – Conclusion – Recapping and Next Steps

What's in a question? More than we might think. I hope I've illustrated that fact throughout this book. We've thought about the nature of questioning. The way it provokes thinking and makes demands on learners. The way the structure of a question influences the kind of thinking it provokes and the kind of learning to which it gives rise.

We've explored a wide range of questioning techniques, all of which can help you to ask better questions or get more out of the question-led interactions you have with your learners. When using the techniques, be prepared for some trial and error. They won't all work like clockwork first time round. You'll need to play around with some of them, test them out, see what happens, and adapt them to suit your approach and that of your learners. But rest assured, there's plenty of ideas packed into the book, giving you lots to get your teeth into.

Let's bring all those techniques together and recap them:

Five specific ways you can open up learning are by:

1) Using the Word 'Might'

2) Reframing Your Questions

3) Digging Deeper with a Second Question

4) Following Up with an 'Else' Question

5) Asking for Examples

Five techniques you can use to get past I don't know are:

1) Using Midwife Questioning

2) Encouraging Learners to use Scrap Paper

3) Prompting Learners

4) Asking: 'What if you did know?'

5) Asking: 'What would we need to know?'

Five ways to elicit better responses are:

1) Using Wait Time

2) Asking Learners to Talk to a Partner

3) Asking Learners to Note Down Their Thoughts

4) Asking: 'Can you explain it to an alien?'

5) Using Ignoramus Questioning

Five ways you can scaffold questions are:

1) Breaking a Question Down into Sub-Questions

2) Providing Answer Options

3) Using a Continuum

4) Using Answer Tokens

5) Clueing

Five techniques connected to open and closed questioning are:

1) Use a series of closed questions to build up to an open question

2) Use Big Picture Open Questions

3) Use Open Questions Connected to Prior Knowledge

4) Use Closed Questions to Check Knowledge

5) Use Closed Questions for Practice Testing

Five creative questioning techniques you can use in the classroom are:

1) 'What if...' Questions

2) Stingray Questions

3) If this is the answer, what might the question be?

4) Word Selection

5) Question Maps

Bloom's Taxonomy takes the core types of thinking learners do in the classroom and puts them in order from simplest to most complex. Each level is more challenging than the last. The six levels are:

- Level 1: Knowledge   **(Simplest)**

- Level 2: Comprehension

- Level 3: Application

- Level 4: Analysis

- Level 5: Synthesis

- Level 6: Evaluation   **(Most Complex)**

You can use Bloom's Taxonomy to come up with questions. Pick the level you think is right for your learner, then use it to develop a question. You can move up or down the taxonomy depending on the response you get.

SOLO Taxonomy sketches out how understanding develops through a series of five levels:

Level 1: Pre-Structural   **(Simplest)**

Level 2: Uni-Structural

Level 3: Multi-Structural

Level 4: Relational

Level 5: Extended Abstract   **(Most Complex)**

Depending where learners are at, you can pose them questions at different levels of the taxonomy, using these to engage them, challenge them and help them to develop their thinking.

When it comes to next steps, my advice is simple. Select a handful of techniques you like the sound of and give them a try. See what happens. If they work, carry on using them. If they don't, ask yourself why. Think about what happened and whether you could change something next time around. Tweak the technique and give it another go. If you believe in the technique (and I believe in all of the techniques in the book) keep trying it and tweaking it until you get the response you're looking for.

Overall, though, have some fun while you're doing it. Enjoy trying out the techniques and thinking about the responses they cause and the thinking they provoke. Questioning is an endlessly fascinating subject. And you are now well set to think critically and creatively about it every time you set foot in a classroom.

Select Bibliography

Anderson, Lorin W.; Krathwohl, David R., (eds), *A taxonomy for learning, teaching, and assessing: A revision of Bloom's taxonomy of educational objectives*. Harlow: Pearson Education, 2014

Black, Paul; Wiliam, Dylan, et al, *Assessment for Learning: Putting it into Practice.* Maidenhead: Open University Press, 2003

Bloom, B. S.; Engelhart, M. D.; Furst, E. J.; Hill, W. H.; Krathwohl, D. R., *Taxonomy of educational objectives: The classification of educational goals. Handbook I: Cognitive domain.* New York: David McKay Company, 1956

Bruner, J., *Acts of Meaning.* Cambridge, Massachusetts: Harvard University Press, 1990

Bruner, J., *Child's Talk: Learning to use Language.* New York: WW Norton & Co. 1983

Bruner, J., *The Culture of Education.* Cambridge, Massachusetts: Harvard University Press, 1996

Dewey, J., Experience and Education (Reprint edition). New York: Touchstone, 1997 [1938]

Donaldson, M., *Children's Minds.* London: Fontana, 1978

Evans, Keith, *Golden Rules of Advocacy.* Oxford: Oxford Higher Education, 2002

Ginnis, Paul, *The Teacher's Toolkit.* Carmarthen: Crown House Publishing, 2002

Mercer, N., *The Guided Construction of Knowledge: talk amongst teachers and learners.* Clevedon: Multilingual Matters, 1995

Mercer, N., *Words and Minds: how we use language to think together.* London: Routledge, 2000

Morley, Ian, *The Devil's Advocate.* London: Sweet & Maxwell, 2009

Petty, Geoff, *Teaching Today: A Practical Guide.* Cheltenham: Nelson Thornes, 2004

Plato, *Five Dialogues: Euthyphro, Apology, Crito, Meno, Phaedo* (2nd edition translated by G. M. A. Grube and revised by John M. Cooper). Indianapolis: Hackett Publishing, 2002

Vygotsky, L., *Mind and Society* (M. Cole, V. John-Steiner, S. Scribner and E. Souberman Eds.). Cambridge, Massachusetts: Harvard University Press, 1978

Vygotsky, L., *Thought and Language* (Revised and edited by Alex Kozulin). Cambridge, Massachusetts: Massachusetts Institute of Technology, 1986

Made in the USA
Lexington, KY
28 May 2018